W9-BWB-335

What's the Weather?

SCHOLASTIC

Children's Press®
A Division of Scholastic Inc.
New York Toronto London Auckland Sydney Mexico City
New Delhi Hong Kong Danbury, Connecticut

Early Childhood Consultants:

Ellen Booth Church
Diane Ohanesian

© 2010 Scholastic Inc.

All rights reserved. Published by Children's Press, an imprint of Scholastic Inc. Published simultaneously in Canada. Printed in China.

SCHOLASTIC, CHILDREN'S PRESS, ROOKIE PRESCHOOL, and associated logos are trademarks and/or registered trademarks of Scholastic Inc.

1 2 3 4 5 6 7 8 9 10 R 19 18 17 16 15 14 13 12 11 10   62

Library of Congress Cataloging-in-Publication Data

What's the Weather?
    p. cm. — (Rookie preschool)
ISBN-13: 978-0-531-24410-4 (lib. bdg.)   ISBN-13: 978-0-531-24585-9 (pbk.)
ISBN-10: 0-531-24410-5 (lib. bdg.)   ISBN-10: 0-531-24585-3 (pbk.)

1. Weather—Juvenile literature. I. Title. II. Series.
QC981.3.R59 2009
551.6 – dc22   2009004777

Rain

Wind

What's the
weather?
Do you know?

Sun

Snow

Splish!

Splish!

Splash
in puddles!

What's the weather?

It's a
rainy
day!

◐ **Rain falls from clouds.**

◐ **Rain helps flowers grow.**

◐ **Rain helps keep grass green.**

Catch!

Catch!

Catch
the wind!

What's the weather?

9

It's a windy day!

Wind helps
carry seeds
from one place
to another.

Wind bends
the branches
of trees.

Wind helps
kites fly.

Play!

Play!

Play
in the snow!

12

What's the weather?

13

It's a
snowy
day!

Snow is white and falls from the sky.

Snow protects plants from freezing.

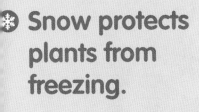

You can make footprints in snow.

See!

See!

See your shadow!

What's the weather?

It's a
sunny day!

☼ The sun helps
flowers grow.

☼ The sun warms
our bodies.

☼ The sun warms
animals.

Some
days are
rainy.

Some days are
windy.

Some days are

snowy.

Some days are
sunny.

What's your favorite kind of weather?

Rookie Storytime Tips

What's the Weather? is an inviting guessing game with visual clues that explores basic types of weather. As you share this book with your child, encourage him or her to take a guess before turning each page that asks, "What's the weather?" Guessing games are not only loads of fun—they are a wonderful way to develop important early critical-thinking skills.

Invite your preschooler to go back through the book and find the following. Along the way, you'll be reinforcing comprehension of basic weather concepts.

What helps flowers grow?

What warms a turtle?

What helps a kite fly?

Look out the window. What's the weather today?